Julia Torres

SPEAK BUSINESS SPANISH

PERFECT YOUR SPOKEN SPANISH FOR WORK

OPPIAN

Published by Oppian Press
Helsinki, 2020

ISBN 978-951-877-154-1

How to use this book

Speaking a foreign language can be daunting, even for somebody who understands spoken language pretty well. Yet being able to converse with others in their native tongue is a vital skill, not least in a business environment.

This book contains 25 useful and unique exercises for advanced learners of Spanish. All exercises are dialogues that take place in a business setting. So grab a friend or a fellow student and start improving your Spanish today!

The way to use the book is simple: each dialogue has two speakers, A and B. Let's say you are A and your partner is B and you want to try dialogue number 4.

First make a copy of the dialogue. You will keep the page Dialogue 4 • A to yourself and give the page Dialogue 4 • B to your partner.

On top of the page you can see a short description of the setting and the speakers. Below that you will see your lines in English. Go ahead and try to say the lines in Spanish. Please remember, that the important thing is to convey the meaning, not to get hung up on individual words.

Your partner will see a Spanish version of your lines on his page, so they can help you with hints if you get stuck or some words are unfamiliar to you.

Likewise, you will see Spanish versions of their lines on your page, so you can help him as well.

After you have completed the exercise, just swap pages and roles. Now it's your turn to be B!

I hope this book will be useful to you and help you be successful in your chosen career.

Julia Torres

DIALOGUE 1 • A

A is a receptionist at a hotel and B is the customer who wants to check in. B wants to make sure the room is quiet and needs further information on the hotel facilities.

A: Good afternoon.

B: Hola. Quisiera registrarme, por favor.

A: Certainly, what is your name?

B: B Jones.

A: Alright, I can see in the computer that you made your booking online so the room has already been paid for. I will however, need a credit card and a form of identification from you so that I can keep them on file for any additional expenses.

B: ¿A qué se refiere con "gastos adicionales"?

A: They are products and services that are not included in the room rate including room service, mini-bar items, internet and movies. We won't charge anything until you check out, however we need to register your method of payment as security.

B: Muy bien. Aquí están mi pasaporte y mi tarjeta de crédito. Me preguntaba qué habitaciones estarán disponibles, porque tengo una reunión a primera hora y le agradecería mucho si pudiera ser una habitación silenciosa.

A: I have a room on the second floor that is very quiet. Unfortunately it does not have a view, but it is far away from the street and the elevators.

B: Está bien. La vista no es importante para mí. ¿Cómo me puedo conectar a la red Wi-Fi?

A: If you open your browser there will be a form asking for your room number and your surname. Once you accept the terms and conditions the service will be added to your credit card charges.

B: ¿Cuándo y dónde se sirve el desayuno?

A: Buffet breakfast is served in the restaurant on the fifth floor from 7am to 9:30 am. However, the restaurant does provide a-la-carte service of breakfast after that.

B: Ok. Gracias por la información.

A: You are very welcome. If you have any further questions just dial 1 on the phone in your room. The elevator is just down the hall, your room is number 206 and it is located on the second floor. I hope that you will enjoy your stay with us.

DIALOGUE 1 • B

A is a receptionist at a hotel and B is the customer who wants to check in. B wants to make sure the room is quiet and needs further information on the hotel facilities.

A: Buenas tardes.

B: Hello. I'd like to check in please.

A: Por supuesto. ¿Cuál es su nombre?

B: B Jones.

A: Muy bien, puedo ver en la computadora que usted realizó su reserva a través de internet, así que su habitación ya está paga. Sin embargo, necesitaré una tarjeta de crédito y algún documento personal para identificarlo y para que queden en nuestros registros en caso de que haya gastos adicionales.

B: What do you mean by "additional expenses"?

A: Son productos y servicios que no están incluidos en la tarifa de la habitación, tales como el servicio a la habitación, artículos del mini-bar, internet y películas. No le cobraremos nada hasta que deje la habitación. Sin embargo, debemos registrar el método de pago como medida de seguridad.

B: That's ok. Here are my passport and credit card. I was wondering which rooms are available because I have an early morning meeting and I would really appreciate it if I could have a quiet room.

A: Tengo una habitación en el segundo piso que es muy silenciosa. Lamentablemente no tiene vista, pero está bien alejada de la calle y de los ascensores.

B: That's fine, the view is not important to me. How can I connect to the Wi-Fi network?

A: Si abre su navegador, encontrará un formulario que le pide su número de habitación y su apellido. Una vez que acepte los términos y condiciones, el servicio se agregará a sus consumos de tarjeta de crédito.

B: When and where will breakfast be served?

A: Se sirve un desayuno buffet en el restaurant del quinto piso, de 7am a 9:30am. Igualmente, luego, el restaurant provee servicio a la carta para el desayuno.

B: Ok. Thank you for the information.

A: No hay de qué. Si llegara a tener alguna otra duda, marque 1 en el teléfono de su habitación. El ascensor está al final del pasillo. Su número de habitación es 206 y queda en el segundo piso. Espero que disfrute su estadía con nosotros.

DIALOGUE 2 • A

A is an assistant at a construction company and B is a business journalist who wants to speak with the company's CEO about the company's latest financial results.

A: Grey Construction, how may I direct your call?

B: Hola, habla B Marks de Business Weekly. En este momento estamos preparando un artículo para describir algunos de los procesos empresariales más notables de la ciudad y nos gustaría solicitar una declaración de su CEO.

A: Our CEO is currently in a meeting and unable to take calls. Would you like to leave a message?

B: ¿Sería posible que usted me dé su número de extensión para que yo pueda llamarlo más tarde? ¿O quizás su dirección de correo electrónico para poder enviarle mis preguntas?

A: I am sorry, but I am unable to disclose that information at this time. However, I would be more than happy to write down some further details and pass them on to him as soon as he becomes available.

B: De acuerdo. Somos una de las revistas comerciales más importantes del sector. Sus últimos reportes financieros han presentado una impresionante mejora y nos gustaría hacerle algunas preguntas sobre cuál ha sido su receta para el éxito.

A: That sounds very interesting. I will pass your details on to our CEO and as soon as I have his answer I will contact you with further details. Could you please provide a phone number that I can reach you on and I will be sure to call you by the end of the day.

B: Si, por supuesto. Mi número es 617 636 5477 y, nuevamente, mi nombre es B Marks.

A: Thank you, I will be in touch this afternoon.

B: Quedo a la espera. Gracias por su ayuda.

DIALOGUE 2 • B

A is an assistant at a construction company and B is a business journalist who wants to speak with the company's CEO about the company's latest financial results.

A: Grey Construction, ¿con quién necesita hablar?

B: Hello, this is B Marks from the Business Weekly. We are currently preparing an article outlining some of the city's' most dramatic business turnarounds and we'd like to request a statement from your CEO.

A: Nuestro CEO está en una reunión ahora y no puede atender llamados. ¿Desearía dejarle un mensaje?

B: Is there any chance that you could give me his extension so that I can call him at a later time? Or perhaps him email address so that I can send him my questions?

A: Lo lamento, pero no me es posible proporcionar esa información. Sin embargo, estaré encantada de tomar nota de los detalles y transmitírselos a él apenas se desocupe.

B: OK. We are one of the most prominent business publications in the area. Your latest financial reports displayed an impressive improvement and we would like to ask a few questions regarding what the recipe for success has been.

A: Eso suena muy interesante. Le transmitiré estos detalles a nuestro CEO y apenas tenga su respuesta, me contactaré con usted con más información. ¿Por favor podría indicarme un número de teléfono donde lo pueda ubicar? Me aseguraré de llamarlo a última hora.

B: Yes of course. My number is 617 636 5477 and once again, my name is B Marks.

A: Muchas gracias, lo llamaré por la tarde.

B: I look forward to it. Thank you for your help.

DIALOGUE 3 • A

A has just missed a flight. B is the airline customer service agent at the airport.

A: Hi, I've just arrived at the airport after my taxi was caught in a traffic jam and realised that I have missed my flight to Munich. Could I please book a seat on the next available flight?

B: Lamento mucho lo ocurrido. Haré lo posible para asistirlo y hacer que este viaje sea menos estresante. ¿Podría darme su pasaporte, por favor?

A: Of course. Here you go.

B: Gracias. Veo aquí que usted realizó la reserva en nuestra oficina de Berlín y la buena noticia es que su boleto "flexible plus" califica para el beneficio de vuelo perdido.

A: What does that mean?

B: Significa que usted no tiene que abonar el precio completo del nuevo boleto. En cambio, se le cobrará una diferencia en la tarifa del pasaje, más una penalidad de reprogramación de 60 euros.

A: That is good news.

B: Lamentablemente, también tengo malas noticias. No hay más vuelos a Munich programados hasta mañana a las 08:10 de la mañana.

A: I guess that I will have to book a seat on that flight then. How much will that cost?

B: Hay un asiento en pasillo disponible en el vuelo de las 08:10 directo a Munich de mañana por la mañana. La tarifa es de 524 euros que son 104 euros más que su tarifa inicial. Esto hará un total de 164 euros, incluyendo la penalidad.

A: OK. Please book the seat for me. Here is my credit card. Also, could you please tell me if there is a good hotel nearby?

B: Hay dos hoteles ubicados en las inmediaciones del aeropuerto. Uno es un Hilton de cuatro estrellas y el otro es una opción más económica. Nosotros les recomendamos el Hilton a nuestros pasajeros porque forma parte de nuestro programa de alianza. Ofrecen un servicio de traslados gratis hacia las terminales de salida y usted recibirá puntos de viajero frecuente cuando realice la reserva.

A: Are you able to make the booking for me from here and how can I get there?

B: Lamentablemente no me es posible realizar la reserva. Sin embargo, cuando vaya hacia la salida, al final del pasillo, verá un escritorio de información. Alguien allí podrá realizar la reserva para usted y hay un taxi justo detrás de las mismas puertas de salida.

A: OK. Thank you very much for all your help.

DIALOGUE 3 • B

A has just missed a flight. B is the airline customer service agent at the airport.

A: Hola, recién llegué al aeropuerto luego de que mi taxi se atascara en un embotellamiento y me doy cuenta de que perdí mi vuelo a Munich. ¿Podría por favor reservarme un asiento en el próximo vuelo disponible?

B: I am very sorry to hear that. I will do my best to assist you and make this journey less stressful! May I have your passport please?

A: Por supuesto. Aquí está.

B: Thank you. I see here that you made your booking at our Berlin office and the good news is that your "flexible plus" ticket fare qualifies for the missed flight feature.

A: ¿Qué significa?

B: This means that you do not have to pay for the full price of the new ticket. Instead, you will be charged for any difference in the fare price plus a 60 euro rescheduling penalty.

A: Qué buena noticia.

B: Unfortunately, I also have bad news. There are no more flights to Munich scheduled until tomorrow morning at 08:10.

A: Calculo que tendré que reservar un asiento en ese vuelo, entonces. ¿Cuánto costará?

B: There is an aisle seat available on the 08:10 flight direct to Munich tomorrow morning. The fare price is 524 euros which is 104 euros more than your initial fare. This will bring your total to 164 euros including the penalty.

A: De acuerdo. Por favor resérveme ese asiento. Aquí está mi tarjeta de crédito. Además, ¿por favor podría indicarme si hay algún buen hotel cerca?

B: There are two hotels located on airport premises. One is a 4-star Hilton and the other is a more budget friendly option. We recommend the Hilton to our passengers because they are part of our alliance program. They offer a free shuttle service to the departures terminal and you receive frequent flyer points when booking.

A: ¿Usted podría realizar la reserva desde aquí y cómo hago para llegar allá?

B: Unfortunately, I am unable to make the booking. However, on your way to the exit at the end of the hall you will see an information desk. Somebody at the desk will be able to make the reservation for you and there is a taxi bay immediately behind the same exit doors.

A: OK. Muchas gracias por toda su ayuda.

DIALOGUE 4 • A

A is on a business trip and wants to rent a car for three days. B is an employee of the car rental company.

A: Hello, I'd like to rent a car and was wondering if you could assist me.

B: Será un placer. ¿Me permitiría por favor su licencia de conducir? ¿El alquiler será a partir de hoy?

A: Yes, I need it immediately and I need it for three days.

B: ¿Piensa devolver el vehículo en este centro o en otro de nuestros centros de devolución nacionales?

A: I will return the car here.

B: ¿Prefiere uno de transmisión manual o automática?

A: Automatic. Also, I would like something that is suitable for business travel. I don't need a large vehicle but I do prefer a 4-door car.

B: Considerando sus necesidades y preferencias, le puedo recomendar un par de opciones que están disponibles en este momento. Un Chrysler o Toyota a 49 dólares por día, o el Nissan a 59 dólares por día. Están todos en nuestro estacionamiento por si los quiere ver.

A: There is no need, I would like to rent the Chrysler please. Does the car come fully insured?

B: Ofrecemos una cobertura de seguros completa por 30 dólares extras y con eso cubrirá todas las colisiones, daños accidentales, etc. hasta un valor de 100.000 dólares. Puede ver más detalles en este folleto.

A: Please sign me up for the complete cover.

B: Por supuesto. El total es de 177 dólares. Si por favor me permite su tarjeta de crédito, haré un bloqueo por este importe, que no será debitado hasta que usted devuelva el vehículo, que puede ser en cualquier momento del jueves entre las 7 am y las 6 pm. Además, por favor observe que se le solicita devolver el auto con el tanque de combustible lleno. Aquí está la documentación, por favor firme esta copia y conserve la otra copia en el auto en todo momento.

A: Thank you for your help.

B: De nada. Enviaré a alguien para que traiga su auto a la entrada en un minuto. ¡Que tenga un maravilloso día y conduzca con cuidado!

DIALOGUE 4 • B

A is on a business trip and wants to rent a car for three days. B is an employee of the car rental company.

A: Hola, me gustaría alquilar un auto y quisiera saber si usted podría ayudarme.

B: It would be my pleasure. May I please see your drivers' license? And will you be renting the vehicle starting today?

A: Si, lo necesito ahora mismo y por tres días.

B: Do you intend to return the vehicle to this centre or to another one of our nationwide drop-off centres?

A: Devolveré el auto aquí.

B: Do you prefer a manual or automatic transmission?

A: Automática. Además, quisiera alguno que sea apropiado para viajes de negocios. No necesito un vehículo grande pero prefiero que tenga cuatro puertas.

B: I've taken your needs and preferences into consideration and I can recommend a couple of options that are currently available. The Chrysler or Toyota at 49 dollars a day or the Nissan for 59 dollars a day. They are all in our caryard if you would like to take a look.

A: No hace falta. Quisiera alquilar el Chrysler por favor. ¿El auto viene con todos los seguros?

B: We offer complete insurance coverage at an extra 30 dollars and that will cover all collisions, accidental damage etc. to a value of 100 thousand dollars. You can see more details in this pamphlet.

A: Por favor regístreme para la cobertura completa.

B: Certainly. Your total comes to 177 dollars. If I may please have your credit card I will place a hold to this amount which will not be deducted until you return the vehicle, which can be any time on Thursday between 7 am and 6 pm. Also, please note that you are required to return the car with the fuel tank refilled. Here is your paperwork, please sign this copy and retain the other copy to keep in the car at all times.

A: Muchas gracias por su ayuda.

B: You are very welcome. I will send somebody to bring your car around to the entrance in a minute. Have a lovely day and drive safely!

DIALOGUE 5 • A

A is a customs and immigration agent at an international border. B is a business visitor.

A: May I see your passport?

B: Si, por supuesto.

A: Do you have a valid visa to enter our country?

B : Si, poseo visa. La puede ver en mi pasaporte.

A: What is the purpose of your visit?

B: Trabajo en una marca de moda internacional y vengo a ofrecer nuestra nueva colección en varios negocios minoristas.

A: How long will you be staying here and where will you be residing?

B: 10 días y me quedaré en el Superb Hotel en Bigtown.

A: Could I see your return ticket and your reservation details if you have them printed please?

B: No tengo mi reserva de hotel impresa. Tengo un correo electrónico de confirmación en mi teléfono celular pero en este momento no tengo acceso a internet.

A: That's ok, the return ticket is fine. How do you intend to finance your time here?

B: Tengo una tarjeta de crédito corporativa y suficiente dinero en efectivo para mis gastos personales.

A: Are you carrying any goods that you plan to distribute or sell while here?

B: No, solo productos de muestra.

A: OK, everything seems to be in order. Welcome and enjoy your stay.

DIALOGUE 5 • B

A is a customs and immigration agent at an international border. B is a business visitor.

A: ¿Me permite su pasaporte?

B: Yes, of course.

A: ¿Usted posee una visa válida para ingresar a nuestro país?

B :   Yes, I have a visa, you will see it in my passport.

A: ¿Cuál es el motivo de su visita?

B: I work for an international fashion label and I am here to offer our new collection to several retail stores.

A: ¿Cuánto tiempo se quedará aquí y dónde estará residiendo?

B: 10 days and I will be staying at the Superb Hotel in Bigtown.

A: ¿Podría ver su boleto de regreso y los detalles de su reserva si los tiene impresos, por favor?

B: I do not have my hotel booking printed, I have the confirmation in an email on my mobile phone but I do not currently have internet access.

A: Muy bien, el boleto de regreso está bien. ¿Cómo tiene pensado financiar su estadía aquí?

B: I have a company credit card and sufficient cash for personal costs.

A: ¿Lleva mercadería que piense distribuir o vender aquí?

B: No, only sample products.

A: OK, todo parece estar en orden. Bienvenido y que disfrute su estadía.

DIALOGUE 6 • A

A is a business traveller whose luggage has disappeared. B is a customer service agent at the airport.

A: Hi, could you please help me? My luggage hasn't arrived on the carousel.

B: Lamento oír eso. ¿Puedo ver su pasaporte, por favor? ¿Y en qué vuelo arribó?

A: The EK420 from Dubai.

B: ¿Llegó directamente desde Dubai o voló en conexión con algún otro destino?

A: I began my journey in Zurich.

B: Hay una posibilidad de que su equipaje no haya llegado a la conexión inicial. Sin embargo, eventualmente llegará aquí. Para poder procesar su reclamo, necesito hacerle algunas preguntas para ayudarnos a identificar sus valijas. ¿Cuántas piezas de equipaje están faltando?

A: Two. I have name tags on both of them.

B: ¿Podría por favor describir las valijas, incluyendo color, material y cualquier estampado o marca

A: They are both Samsonite, plain black bags. The name tags are bright red tags. I'm not sure about the dimensions, they are large suitcases.

B: Thank you. Please fill out this form stating the address to which you would like us to deliver your luggage once it arrives and sign the bottom once you have read the terms and conditions. Make sure that you also provide a local phone number so that we can reach you if any issues arise.

A: When can I expect my bags to arrive?

B: Haremos lo posible por entregarlas dentro de las próximas 72 horas.

A: OK, thank you.

DIALOGUE 6 • B

A is a business traveller whose luggage has disappeared. B is a customer service agent at the airport.

A: Hola, ¿podría usted ayudarme, por favor? Mi equipaje no llegó en la cinta transportadora.

B: I am sorry to hear that. Can I see your passport, please? And which flight did you arrive on?

A: En el EK420 desde Dubai.

B: Did you arrive directly from Dubai or did your flight connect from another destination?

A: Comencé mi viaje en Zurich.

B: There is a possibility that your luggage did not make the initial connection, however it will eventually arrive here. In order to process this claim I will need to ask you a few questions to help us identify your bags. How many pieces of luggage are missing?

A: Dos. Hay identificación en las dos.

B: Could you please describe the bags including their size, colour, material and any patterns or brand names?

A: Ambas son valijas Samsonite, negras lisas. Las etiquetas identificadoras son rojo brillante. No estoy seguro sobre las dimensiones, son valijas grandes.

B: Thank you. Please fill out this form stating the address to which you would like us to deliver your luggage once it arrives and sign the bottom once you have read the terms and conditions. Make sure that you also provide a local phone number so that we can reach you if any issues arise.

A: ¿Cuándo estima que llegarían mis valijas?

B: We will do our best to deliver them within the next 72 hours.

A: OK, gracias.

DIALOGUE 7 • A

A is an art director for a graphic design firm, and B is her client. B asks A to make some tweaks in the new marketing material, and wants to know if she can get the work done by tomorrow.

A: Hi B. Thanks for the draft marketing materials you sent through yesterday afternoon. We love the design and layout of everything, and the new logo is exactly what we were looking for. We're not so sure about the colour scheme in the corporate brochure though, and some of the images aren't quite right for our brand either.

B: OK, parece que necesitamos hacer algunos ajustes, entonces. ¿Sobre qué imágenes no están del todo seguros?

A: The ones on pages 3, 9 and 11. The rest are fine, but we'd rather use something a bit more targeted on these pages, to better illustrate the messages in the copy. Perhaps some shots of our products, or members of our sales team meeting with clients. I can give you access to our online image library; I'm sure you'll be able to find some suitable shots in there.

B: De acuerdo, por supuesto. Por favor envíame el hipervínculo y las miraré ya mismo. ¿Y cuál sería su idea sobre el esquema de colores? ¿Preferirían algo más sutil o directamente todos colores diferentes?

A: We do like the colours, but the shades are a bit too bold for us. We're targeting a business audience and we want a more professional look. Could you have them toned down a bit please? I'll send you our branding style guide so you can see which pantones we usually use.

B: Eso será muy útil, muchas gracias.

A: OK great. That's all really, just those tweaks to make. We've got to get drafts of these documents in front of the directors on Wednesday morning for approval. Is there any chance you can prioritise these changes please, and send me through an updated version of the brochure by tomorrow?

B: Si, ciertamente puedo hacerlo, siempre que usted me pueda enviar esa guía de estilo y el hipervínculo para la biblioteca de imágenes hoy por la mañana.

A: Great, thanks. I'll email them to you right away. Call me if you need any clarification. I look forward to seeing the final draft tomorrow.

B: Gracias, A. Adiós.

DIALOGUE 7 • B

A is an art director for a graphic design firm, and B is her client. B asks A to make some tweaks in the new marketing material, and wants to know if she can get the work done by tomorrow.

A: HolaB. Gracias por el material de promoción en borrador que me enviaste ayer por la tarde. Nos encantó el diseño y la disposición de todo, y el nuevo logo es exactamente lo que estábamos buscando. No estamos seguros sobre el esquema de colores en el folleto corporativo, igualmente, y algunas de las imágenes no están del todo bien para nuestra marca tampoco.

B: OK, it sounds like we need to make some adjustments then. Which images are you uncertain about?

A: Las de las páginas 3, 9 y 11. Las demás están bien, pero preferiríamos usar algo un poco más específico en esas páginas, para ilustrar mejor los mensajes en la copia. Tal vez algunas tomas de nuestros productos, o de miembros de nuestro equipo de ventas reuniéndose con clientes. Te puedo dar acceso a nuestra biblioteca de imágenes en línea. Estoy seguro de que podrás encontrar fotos más apropiadas ahí.

B: OK, of course. Please email me the link and I'll look through them right away. So what are your thoughts on the colour scheme? Would you prefer something more subtle, or do you want different colours altogether?

A: Nos gustan los colores pero las sombras son un poco gruesas para nosotros. Estamos apuntando a una audiencia de negocios y queremos una imagen un poco más profesional. ¿Podrías bajarles un poco el tono, por favor? Te enviaré nuestra guía de estilo de marca para que puedas ver cuáles son los pantones que utilizamos habitualmente.

B: That would be really helpful. Thank you.

A: OK genial. Eso es todo, entonces. Sólo hacer esas modificaciones. Tenemos que llevarles borradores de estos documentos a nuestros directores el miércoles a la mañana para que los aprueben. ¿Hay alguna posibilidad de que puedas priorizar estos cambios, por favor, y enviarme una versión actualizada del folleto para mañana?

B: Yes, I can definitely do that, provided that you can get that style guide and the link for the image library over to me this morning.

A: Genial, gracias. Te las enviaré por correo electrónico ya mismo. Llámame si necesitas alguna aclaración. Aguardo la versión final para mañana.

B: Thanks A. Bye for now.

DIALOGUE 8 • A

A is on his way to a business meeting with B, but his car has broken down. A calls B to apologise and asks if B wants to reschedule the meeting.

A: Hi B, this is A. I'm so sorry, but I'm running late for our meeting this morning. My car has broken down on the highway, and I'm waiting for roadside assistance.

B: Qué desafortunado. ¿Tienes idea cuánto tiempo demorará?

A: Apparently the response time is up to an hour, so even if they can get it running right away I doubt I could be there until 1 pm at the earliest. Would it suit you to meet this afternoon instead, or would you prefer to reschedule.

B: Espera un momento, déjame ver mi agenda. La pondré en la pantalla.

A: OK, thanks

B: Oh, parece que vendrá un nuevo cliente después del almuerzo, así que lamento que no podré verte esta tarde. Tendremos que posponerlo para otro día. Pero tenemos algunos asuntos urgentes para cubrir, así que hagámoslo lo antes posible.

A: Yes, we need to go over those year-end procedures as soon as possible, and review progress on the marketing project. The deadline is only two weeks away so we've no time to waste. Are you free tomorrow morning?

B: Parece que estaré bastante ocupado pero te puedo hacer un hueco si puede ser temprano. ¿Qué te parece un desayuno a las 8am? No estoy seguro de si alguno de mis colegas se nos podrá unir a esa hora, pero yo les puedo pasar la información luego.

A: Yes, I can make 8 am tomorrow. Do you want to meet at your offices?

B: Si, aunque no habrá nadie en recepción a esa hora. ¿Puedes por favor llamarme al celular cuando llegues, así bajo a abrirte? ¿Tienes el número?

A: Yes, I do. Thanks so much for your flexibility. I'll see you in the morning.

B: Gracias. Nos vemos.

DIALOGUE 8 • B

A is on his way to a business meeting with B, but his car has broken down. A calls B to apologise and asks if B wants to reschedule the meeting.

A: Hola B, habla A. Lo lamento tanto, pero estoy demorado para nuestra reunión de esta mañana. Mi auto se rompió en la autopista y estoy esperando a la asistencia en ruta.

B: That's frustrating. Have you any idea how long you'll be?

A: Aparentemente el tiempo de repuesta es de hasta una hora, así que aunque lo hagan arrancar ahí mismo, dudo que pueda llegar allá antes de la 1pm como temprano. ¿Te convendría que nos reunamos esta tarde, en cambio, o preferirías reprogramar

B: Hang on. Let me check my diary. I'll just pull it up on my screen.

A: De acuerdo, gracias.

B: It looks like we've got a new client coming in after lunch, so I'm afraid I won't be able to see you this afternoon. We'll have to move it to another day. But we've got some quite urgent matters to cover, so let's make it as soon as possible.

A: Si, tenemos que revisar esos procedimientos de fin de año lo antes posible, y ver el progreso del proyecto de marketing. La fecha límite es dentro de apenas dos semanas así que no tenemos tiempo que perder. ¿Estás libre mañana a la mañana?

B: It's looking quite busy, but I could squeeze you in if you can make it early. How about a breakfast meeting at 8 am? I'm not sure if any of my colleagues will be able to join us at that hour, but I can always brief them afterwards.

A: Si, puedo hacerlo a las 8am mañana. ¿Quieres que nos reunamos en tu oficina?

B: Yes, although reception won't be manned at that hour. Can you please call me on my mobile when you get here, and I'll come down and let you in. You have the number?

A: Si, lo tengo. Muchas gracias por la flexibilidad. Nos vemos a la mañana.

B: Thanks. See you then.

DIALOGUE 9 • A

A calls the company helpline because she cannot log into her online account. B is the customer care specialist helping her. They figure out that A has caps lock on her keyboard and that's why her password is not accepted.

A: IT helpline. This is A speaking. How can I help you today?

B: Hola A. Mi nombre es B y trabajo en el departamento de Cuentas. Hace diez minutos que estoy tratando de ingresar a mi cuenta de la intranet de la empresa, pero me rechaza la contraseña. Estoy segura de que es la correcta y ayer funcionaba bien, así que no puedo darme cuenta qué está pasando. Ahora salió un mensaje que dice que me bloquearon. ¿Me podría ayudar?

A: OK B, let's take a look. Can you give me your surname please so I can find you on the system?

B: Es Smith.

A: Ah yes. I've found you. And can you tell me what username you've typed in?

B: Aguarde, déjeme revisar. Ese campo se autocomplete así que no lo tengo que tipear todas las veces… Ok, es asmith, luego arroba, luego la empresa, punto com. Nunca lo cambio así que estoy segura de que está bien.

A: OK, yes, that's the right format, so that's not the problem. I can see that you've made several log-on attempts in the last quarter of an hour. You've exceeded the maximum number – for security reasons you get locked out after 5.

B: ¿Qué puedo hacer?

A: Don't worry, I can reset it from here. I'll give you a temporary password so you can log on, but you'll need to change that immediately, ok?

B: Si. ¿Cuál es la nueva contraseña?

A: I've reset it to 'smith', all lower case. Can you try it?

B: La estoy tipeando ahora. ¡No! ¡Me la rechazó de nuevo!

A: It's case sensitive. Perhaps your Caps Lock is on. Could you please check?

B: ¡Oh! ¡Lo está! Ese debe haber sido el problema todo el tiempo. Ingresaré la nueva contraseña de nuevo… Si, ¡ingresé! Gracias.

A: That's a pleasure. Glad I could help. Don't forget to choose a new password immediately. Is there anything else I can help you with today?

B: No, gracias A. Realmente le agradezco su ayuda.

DIALOGUE 9 • B

A calls the company helpline because she cannot log into her online account. B is the customer care specialist helping her. They figure out that A has caps lock on her keyboard and that's why her password is not accepted.

A: Línea de asistencia de sistemas. Habla A. ¿En qué lo puedo ayudar el día de hoy?

B: Hi A. My name's B and I work in the Accounts department. I've been trying for ten minutes to log onto my account on the company intranet, but it keeps rejecting my password. I'm sure it's the right one, and it worked fine yesterday so I can't figure out what's going on. Now I've got a message saying I've been locked out. Can you help?

A: OK B, echemos un vistazo. ¿Me podría indicar su apellido, por favor, así la ubico en el sistema?

B: It's Smith.

A: Ah, sí, la encontré. ¿Y me podría decir qué nombre de usuario ingresó?

B: Hang on let me check. There's an autofill on that field so I don't have to type it in every time… OK, It's bsmith, then an 'at' sign, then company dot com. I never change it though, so I'm sure its right.

A: OK, si, ese es el formato correcto así que ese no es el problema. Veo que usted ha realizado varios intentos para ingresar en el último cuarto de hora. Se excedió de la cantidad máxima. Por razones de seguridad, se bloquea después de cinco intentos.

B: So what can I do?

A: No se preocupe, lo puedo resetear desde aquí. Le daré una contraseña temporaria para que pueda ingresar, pero la tendrá que cambiar enseguida, ¿de acuerdo?

B: Sure. What's the new password?

A: La modifiqué a 'smith', todo en minúscula. ¿Puede intentar con esa?

B: Typing it in now. No! It rejected me again!

A: Es sensible a las mayúsculas. Tal vez está activado su "Caps Lock". ¿Podría fijarse?

B: Oh! It is! That must have been the problem all along. I'll try the new password again… Yes, I'm in! Thank you.

A: Es un placer. Me alegro de haberla ayudado. No olvide elegir una nueva contraseña enseguida. ¿Hay algo más con lo que la pueda ayudar hoy?

B: No, thanks A. I really appreciate your help. Bye.

DIALOGUE 10 • A

A calls B to find out if B is happy with the widgets his business purchased from A's company some time ago. B has no complaints about the product, but notes that the shipping company that A used were not quite as punctual as they should have been. A promises to use another shipping company next time.

A: Hi B. This is A from Super Widgets. This is just a courtesy call to make sure you're happy with the consignment of extra wide widgets you bought from us last month. Were you able to install them ok?

B: Hey A. Gracias por su llamado. Los widgets están muy bien, muchas gracias. La instalación no tuvo problemas, gracias, y a todos les parecieron muy fáciles de usar. Hicimos algunos llamados a su equipo de soporte durante los primeros días, pero fueron muy serviciales, y los manuales de instrucciones que vinieron son muy completos.

A: Oh that's great to hear. So they are performing as you'd hoped?

B: Absolutamente. El producto es fantástico y los resultados son justo los que esperábamos. El departamento completo está operando en forma más eficiente y nuestra productividad ha aumentado este mes.

A: That's excellent feedback. Thank you! I'm so glad you're happy with them. So overall, were you happy with your customer experience at Super Widgets?

B: Si, completamente. Ya que pregunta, hubo una sola cosa desalentadora.

A: I'm sorry to hear that! What was it?

B: Bueno, como usted sabe, estábamos un poco apurados por actualizar nuestros sistemas y esperábamos recibir las herramientas dentro de una semana. Nos quedamos impresionados con la velocidad con la que procesaron nuestra orden, pero pasaron más de diez días desde que nos mandaron el aviso de envío hasta que recibimos el paquete. Nos hizo demorar la fecha de lanzamiento y el transporte no nos dio ninguna explicación por la demora.

A: Oh I'm so sorry! That's not at all consistent with our service standards and I'm very disappointed to hear it. I'll start an investigation immediately to find out what happened, and we'll definitely use another shipping company from now on.

B: Fantástico, gracias. Se lo agradezco mucho y también por la llamada. Estaremos en contacto en el próximo trimestre cuando comencemos la fase siguiente de la actualización de los sistemas.

A: Thanks. I'll look forward to meeting with you then to find out how we can help.

DIALOGUE 10 • B

A calls B to find out if B is happy with the widgets his business purchased from A's company some time ago. B has no complaints about the product, but notes that the shipping company that A used were not quite as punctual as they should have been. A promises to use another shipping company next time.

A: Hola B. Habla A de Super Widgets. Esta es una llamada de cortesía para asegurarme de que esté conformes con el envío de widgets extra anchos que nos compró el mes pasado. ¿Pudo instalarlos correctamente?

B: Hey A. Thanks for your call. The widgets are great, thanks. The installation was seamless, thanks, and everyone has found them very easy to use. We made a few calls to your support team in the first few days but they were really helpful, and the instruction manuals you provided with them are very thorough.

A: Oh qué bueno saber eso. ¿Así que están funcionando como usted esperaba?

B: Absolutely. The product is great and the outcome has been just what we were hoping for. The entire department is operating more efficiently and our productivity has been right up this month.

A: Son comentarios excelentes. ¡Gracias! Me alegro mucho de que estén conformes. Así que, en resumen, ¿está satisfecho con su experiencia como cliente en Super Widgets?

B: Yes, on the whole. Since you're asking there was one disappointing thing though.

A: Oh, lo lamento, ¿qué cosa?

B: Well as you know, we were in a bit of a hurry to upgrade our systems and we had expected to receive the widgets within a week. We were very impressed with how fast you processed our order – but it took more than 10 days from when you sent us the shipping notice before the consignment got delivered. It held up our launch date and the courier couldn't give any explanation for the delay at all.

A: Oh, ¡lo lamento tanto! Eso no es para nada coherente con nuestros estándares de servicio y lamento mucho enterarme. Voy a comenzar una investigación inmediatamente para descubrir qué pasó, y definitivamente utilizaremos otra empresa de transporte desde ahora en adelante.

B: Great, thanks. I appreciate that, and the follow up call. We'll be in touch next quarter when we start on the next phase of system upgrades.

A: Gracias. Espero con interés reunirme con usted para saber cómo ayudarlos.

DIALOGUE 11 • A

A is a software developer and B is his manager. There is a critical software bug in the latest build that A has submitted and it has crashed B's computer. A promises to come over and sort things out asap.

A: Hi B, it's A. I've just tried to run the latest version of that finance program you're working on, and it's crashed my computer. It looks like there was a critical bug of some sort in the build you submitted this morning.

B: ¡Oh, no! Lo siento mucho. Lo he testeado bastante a fondo en mi estación antes de enviarlo, y funcionó como un reloj. ¿Qué sucedió exactamente?

A: The installation was quick and straightforward, but it crashed about 2 minutes after I started to run it. I was able to log in ok and access the main menu and setting pages, but as soon as I tried to load the bookkeeping module it just froze. My entire system is completely locked up now; it won't even shut down or restart.

B: Dios mío. Debe estar interactuando de manera adversa con algunos de los otros programas en su PC. Usted tiene algún especialista de recursos humanos y de aplicaciones estratégicas, ¿no? Voy a tener que hacer algunas pruebas de diagnóstico para buscar los problemas de integración.

A: Ok, can you come and do that right away please? I have a budget report to prepare for the management team meeting this afternoon, so I need my system back online urgently. There's some sensitive data I need to retrieve for the report, and I have some unsaved work I really don't want to lose.

B: Sí, iré allí de inmediato para ejecutar esas pruebas. Mientras tanto, voy a clonar su perfil y lo configuraré en otra PC para que pueda trabajar hasta que yo pueda realizar estas pruebas y reiniciado su nuevo sistema. Una vez que sepa cuál es el problema, voy a empezar a trabajar en un parche.

A: Ok, thanks.

DIALOGUE 11 • B

A is a software developer and B is his manager. There is a critical software bug in the latest build that A has submitted and it has crashed B's computer. A promises to come over and sort things out asap.

A: Hola B, habla A. Recién intenté ejecutar la última versión de ese programa de finanzas en el que estás trabajando, y se dañó mi computadora. Parece que había una falla crítica de algún tipo en la versión que me enviaste esta mañana.

B: Oh no! I'm so sorry. I tested it pretty thoroughly at my station before I submitted it, and it ran like clockwork. What happened exactly?

A: La instalación fue rápida y directa, pero se dañó cerca de 2 minutos después de empezar a ejecutarlo. Pude entrar bien y acceder al menú principal y las páginas de configuración, pero apenas traté de cargar el módulo de contabilidad, se tildó. Todo mi sistema está completamente bloqueado ahora; ni siquiera se apaga ni reinicia.

B: Oh dear. It must be interacting adversely with some of the other software on your pc. You have some specialist HR management and strategy applications don't you? I'll need to run some diagnostic tests to look for integration issues.

A: Bueno, ¿puede venir y hacerlo de inmediato, por favor? Tengo que preparar un informe de presupuesto para la reunión del equipo de gestión de esta tarde, así que necesito mi sistema de nuevo en línea con urgencia. Hay algunos datos sensibles que necesito recuperar para el informe, y tengo algo de trabajo no guardado que realmente no quiero perder.

B: Right, I'll come over there straight away and run those tests. In the meantime I'll clone your profile and set you up on another PC so you can work until I can run these tests and get your system rebooted. Once I know what the problem is I'll start work on a patch.

A: Ok, gracias.

DIALOGUE 12 • A

A is a visitor who has an appointment at the marketing department. B is the receptionist who will greet him at the lobby and issue him a visitor pass.

A: Good morning sir. Welcome to Practice Corporation. How can I help you this morning?

B: Hola. Mi nombre es B Jones. Estoy aquí para una reunión con Jack Smith en el departamento de marketing. Me temo que llego un poco temprano.

A: Oh yes, your name is here on our authorised visitors list. I'll just print you out a visitor's pass, so that security will let you through. Could you please fill out your details and sign the visitors' register, just in this box here? The sign in time is 10.47am.

B: Sí, no hay problema. ¿Me podría decir si alguien más ha llegado para la reunión?

A: No, you're the first to arrive, but I see from our schedule that it doesn't start until 11.30 am. I'll just call up and let Mr Smith know that you're here.

B: Muy bien, gracias.

A: Oh, I'm sorry. Mr Smith's secretary informs me he's still tied up in his previous meeting but she'll inform him that you're here. I'm afraid there's another meeting taking place in the conference room at the moment, so I wonder if you'd mind taking a seat down here in the lobby for the moment.

B: No hay problema, esperaré allí. ¿Tiene wifi que pueda usar, así puedo trabajar mientras espero?

A: Yes, certainly. Here's the network name and access password. Would you like a cup of tea or coffee while you wait?

B: No, gracias, pero me encantaría un vaso de agua por favor. Y ¿podría decirme dónde está el baño de caballeros?

A: Yes it's just over there through that door behind that screen. I'll have a jug of water brought out to you right away, and just let me know if there's anything else you need.

B: Se lo agradezco. Gracias.

DIALOGUE 12 • B

A is a visitor who has an appointment at the marketing department. B is the receptionist who will greet him at the lobby and issue him a visitor pass.

A: Buenos días señor. Bienvenido a Practice Corporation. ¿Cómo puedo ayudarlo esta mañana?

B: Hi. My name's B Jones. I'm here for a meeting with Jack Smith in the marketing department. I'm afraid I'm running a bit early.

A: Oh sí, su nombre está aquí en la lista de nuestros visitantes autorizados, Sr. Jones. Voy a imprimir un pase de visitante, así la seguridad lo dejará pasar. ¿Podría usted por favor completar sus datos y firmar el registro de visitantes, en este cuadro de aquí? El horario es 10.47am.

B: Yes, no problem. Could you please tell me whether anyone else has arrived for the meeting yet?

A: No, usted es el primero en llegar, pero veo en nuestro cronograma que no comenzará hasta las 11.30 horas. Voy a llamar y le avisaré al Sr. Smith que usted está aquí.

B: Great, thanks.

A: Oh, lo siento. La secretaria del Sr. Smith me informa que él todavía está en su reunión anterior, pero ella le informará que usted está aquí. Me temo que hay otra reunión en la sala de conferencias en este momento, así que ¿le molestaría tomar asiento aquí abajo en el vestíbulo por el momento?

B: No problem, I'll just wait over there. Do you have wifi I can use, so I can work while I'm waiting?

A: Sí, por supuesto. Aquí está el nombre de la red y la contraseña de acceso. ¿Quisiera una taza de té o café mientras espera?

B: No thanks, but I'd love a drink of water please. And could you please tell me where the men's room is?

A: Sí, está justo allí, a través de esa puerta detrás de esa pantalla. Le haré traer una jarra de agua de inmediato, Sr. Jones, y avíseme si hay algo más necesite.

B: I appreciate it. Thank you.

DIALOGUE 13 • A

A and B and on their way to pitch a new product to a potential customer. They talk about their strategy and agree that B should take the lead and A should help with the technical details.

A: The taxi's here. Are you ready to go? Got everything?

B   Sí, está todo listo. Tengo todos los folletos de productos y las especificaciones técnicas aquí, además de la hoja informativa que me pediste que agregara.

A: Great. What about that consumer research the marketing team were working on. Did they get it to you in time?

B: Sí, y también tengo un archivo de la cobertura mediática de Jenny de Relaciones Públicas. Se ve bastante impresionante; estamos recibiendo algunos comentarios muy positivos de los clientes y de comentaristas de la industria.

A: Great, that will really support our pitch. These guys are quite cautious; they'll want some compelling evidence that the product lives up to our claims. So, let's talk strategy. How shall we handle this one?

B: Bueno, ellos han estado lidiando sólo contigo hasta ahora, así que tiene sentido que tú tomes la delantera. ¿Tú sabes quién va a estar en la reunión?

A: I've only met with Greg and Julie so far. They seem keen but the decision isn't in their hands. Their manager Phil will be there this morning, and the department head too I think. She's the one we'll have to convince.

B: OK. Bueno, ya conoces el terreno de juego por todos lados. ¿Por qué no te dejo a tí la mayor parte de la explicación, y yo te apoyo en los detalles? He estado estudiando estas especificaciones y los datos de los consumidores para poder aportar si tú necesitas detalles y números. Tengo todos los últimos datos de los usuarios y las proyecciones en mi computadora portátil también, en caso de que las pidan.

A: Excellent. And what about the product demo? I think you'd better run that, since you'll be able to answer any questions that come up.

B: Está todo listo para llevar en mi computadora portátil.

A: Great. I think that's everything covered off. Let's go.

DIALOGUE 13 • B

A and B and on their way to pitch a new product to a potential customer. They talk about their strategy and agree that B should take the lead and A should help with the technical details.

A: El taxi está aquí. ¿Estás listo para ir? ¿Tienes todo?

B   Yes, it's all ready. I've got all the product brochures and technical specifications right here, plus that fact sheet you asked me to put together.

A: Fantástico. Qué hay de la investigación de los consumidores en la que estaba trabajando el equipo de marketing, ¿consiguieron entregártela a tiempo?

B: Yes, and I've also got a file of media coverage from Jenny in PR. It's looking quite impressive; we're getting some very positive reviews from both customers and industry commentators.

A: Genial, eso realmente apoyará nuestra muestra. Estos hombres son muy cautelosos; van a querer alguna evidencia convincente de que el producto hace honor a nuestras afirmaciones. Por lo tanto, vamos a hablar de estrategia. ¿Cómo vamos a manejar esto?

B: Well they've only been dealing with you up to now, so it makes sense that you take the lead. Do you know who's going to be at the meeting?

A: Yo sólo me he reunido con Greg y Julie hasta ahora. Parecen entusiasmados, pero la decisión no está en sus manos. Su gerente Phil estará ahí esta mañana, y el jefe de departamento también, creo. Ella es a quien vamos a tener que convencer.

B: OK. Well you know the pitch inside out. Why don't I leave most of the talking to you, and just back you up on the specifics? I've been studying these specs and the consumer data so I can jump in if you need details and numbers. I've got all the latest user figures and projections on my laptop too, in case they ask for them.

A: Excelente. ¿Y qué pasa con la demostración del producto? Creo que será mejor que tú hagas eso, puesto que tú serás capaz de responder cualquier pregunta que se presente.

B: Sure. It's all ready to go on my laptop.

A: Genial. Creo que está todo cubierto. Vamos.

DIALOGUE 14 • A

A is going to launch a new catering business. B is a freelance website developer. A calls to find out how much a professional website would cost her and how quickly it could be done.

A: Web Solutions, A Jackson speaking.

B: Hola A. Mi nombre es B. Necesito un sitio web y acabo de encontrar sus datos en línea. Me gustaría tener una charla con usted acerca de un posible diseño de un sitio para mí. ¿Estaría usted interesado en darme una cotización?

A: Sure. What sort of thing are you looking for?

B: Bueno, yo estoy a punto de lanzar un nuevo negocio de catering y necesito promoverlo. Nos especializamos en banquetes veganos, por lo que queremos un aspecto muy fresco, con muchas imágenes de los alimentos y los ingredientes.

A: OK. Have you got photos already or would you need me to source the images?

B: Acabo de realizar una sesión de fotos profesional así que yo proveeré todas las fotos. También tenemos un poco de trabajo hecho en la marca, así que le puedo dar algunas pautas para el diseño.

A: OK great. So the costs will depend on how complex the layout of the site needs to be. Have you any thoughts on what you want to include?

B: Bueno, tendrá que tener un mapa que muestre las áreas que servimos. También necesitaremos unas cuantas páginas para hablar de lo que hacemos y el tipo de ingredientes que utilizamos, además de algunos ejemplos de menús. También quiero una sección de blog, con enlaces a todos nuestros medios de comunicación social - Pinterest, Instagram, Facebook, etc.

A: OK, that's all quite straightforward. Do you need the site to take bookings, or just encourage people to get in touch with their enquiries?

B: Oh, no, nosotros nos encargaremos de las reservas directamente con los clientes, por lo que sólo queremos que se contacten con nosotros, por teléfono o correo electrónico.

A: Right. That gives me enough to work on. I can put a quote together for you and email it through by Friday. Is that ok?

B: Sí, eso está bien. Y, ¿cuál es su capacidad en este momento? ¿Qué tan rápido cree que podría completar el trabajo?

A: I'm just finishing up another project, but if you decide to go ahead I could make a start towards the middle of next week. I'll include a rough timeline and a suggested site map with my quote. Does that work for you?

B: Sí, es fantástico. Le daré mi dirección de correo electrónico ahora.

DIALOGUE 14 • B

A is going to launch a new catering business. B is a freelance website developer. A calls to find out how much a professional website would cost her and how quickly it could be done.

A: Web Solutions, habla A Jackson.

B: Hi A. My name is B. I need a website and I've just found your details online. I'd like to have a chat to you about maybe building a site for me. Would you be interested in giving me a quote?

A: Claro. ¿Qué tipo de página está buscando?

B: Well I'm about to launch a new catering business and I need to promote it. We specialise in vegan banquets so we want a really fresh look and feel, with lots of images of the food and ingredients.

A: OK. ¿Usted ya tiene fotos o necesita que yo provea las imágenes?

B: We've just had a professional photoshoot done so I'll provide all the pictures. We've had some work done on branding too so I can give you some guidelines for the design.

A: OK genial. Entonces los costos dependerán de la complejidad del diseño del sitio. ¿Tiene alguna idea de lo que quiere incluir?

B: Well there will need to be a map showing which areas we service. We'll also need a few pages to talk about what we do and the kind of ingredients we use, plus some sample menus. I also want a blog section, with links to all our social media feeds – Pinterest, Instagram, Facebook etc.

A: Bueno, eso es todo bastante sencillo. ¿Necesita que el sitio pueda tomar reservas, o simplemente que anime a la gente a ponerse en contacto a través de sus consultas?

B: Oh no, we'll handle the bookings directly with the clients, so we just want them to contact us, by phone or email.

A: Bien. Eso me da suficiente para empezar a trabajar. Puedo prepararle una cotización y enviarla por correo electrónico este viernes. ¿Está bien?

B: Yes that's fine. And what's your capacity like at the moment? How quickly do you think could you complete the work?

A: Justo estoy terminando otro proyecto, pero si usted decide seguir adelante, yo podría comenzar hacia mediados de la próxima semana. Voy a incluir una línea de tiempo aproximada y un mapa del sitio sugerido con mi cotización. ¿Eso le parece apropiado?

B: Yes that's great. I'll give you my email address now.

DIALOGUE 15 • A

A is the office manager for a legal firm and B works for an electronics retailer. A needs to buy tablets for all the professionals in the firm and calls B to negotiate a special rate for a bulk purchase of the devices.

A: Smith Electronics, this is A. How can I help?

B: Hola A. Mi nombre es B. Estoy llamando desde la Firma de Contadores Generales y estoy interesado en comprar unas tabletas para nuestro equipo profesional.

A: I can definitely help you with that. How many do you need?

B: 14. También necesitamos cubiertas protectoras y teclados inalámbricos. ¿Ustedes los venden?

A: Yes we stock the covers and keyboards too. I'm not sure if we could do 14 in the same colour though. Does that matter?

B: No, en absoluto. Todos los colores están bien.

A: OK great. So do you have a particular brand of tablet in mind? What sort of price range are you looking for?

B: Queremos algo de gama media que funcione bien con las aplicaciones de Microsoft Office, así nuestros profesionales pueden utilizarlas cuando están fuera, trabajando en las oficinas de los clientes. Me gustaría conocer su recomendación sobre las marcas.

A: Well we've got several that will meet your needs, and two of those are on sale at the moment, so you'll get a good deal. If you give me your email address I'll send you through the product specs right now.

B: Bien, muchas gracias. ¿Y nos puede ofrecer un precio de descuento, ya que estamos pensando en comprar al por mayor?

A: Yes of course. I'm not sure how much I can discount the tablets as they're already on sale, but I'll see what I can do. And I can certainly offer you a special price on all the accessories. How are you planning to pay?

B: Tenemos una cuenta corporativa con ustedes. ¿Me podría enviar un presupuesto por escrito por favor, así puedo preparar una orden de compra?

A: Yes, sure. I'll email these product specifications to you now. Once you decide which type you want just call back and let me know, and I'll put the quote together right away.

B: Excelente. Gracias A.

DIALOGUE 15 • B

A is the office manager for a legal firm and B works for an electronics retailer. A needs to buy tablets for all the professionals in the firm and calls B to negotiate a special rate for a bulk purchase of the devices.

A: Smith Electronics, habla A. ¿En qué lo puedo ayudar?

B: Hi A. My name is B. I'm calling from the General Accounting Firm and I'm looking to buy some tablets for our professional team.

A: Definitivamente lo puedo ayudar con eso. ¿Cuántas necesita?

B: 14. We also need protective covers and wireless keyboards. Do you sell those?

A: Sí, tenemos en stock las cubiertas y teclados también. Sin embargo, no estoy seguro de si podremos tener 14 en el mismo color. ¿Eso es importante?

B: Not at all. Any colours are fine.

A: OK fantástico. ¿Tiene en mente alguna marca de tableta en particular? ¿Qué tipo de rango de precios es lo que busca?

B: We want something mid-range that will run Microsoft Office applications well, so our professionals can use them when they're out working at clients' offices. I'm happy to take your recommendation on the brand.

A: Bueno, tenemos varias que se adaptan a sus necesidades, y dos de ellas están en promoción en este momento, de manera que obtendrá un buen precio. Si me da su dirección de correo electrónico le enviaré las especificaciones de producto ya mismo.

B: Great, thank you. And can you offer us a discount price, since we're planning to buy in bulk?

A: Sí, por supuesto. No estoy seguro de cuánto puedo descontar de las tabletas, ya que ya están en promoción, pero voy a ver qué puedo hacer. Y ciertamente le puedo ofrecer un precio especial para todos los accesorios. ¿Cómo planea pagar?

B: We have a corporate account with you. Can you provide a written quote please, so I can raise a purchase order?

A: Sí, seguro. Le enviaré estas especificaciones de producto por correo electrónico ahora mismo. Una vez que decida cuál quiere, por favor llámeme de nuevo y hágamelo saber, así haré la cotización de inmediato.

B: Excellent. Thank you A.

DIALOGUE 16 • A

A is a freelance writer who is working on a project for B. She calls B to let him know that the first piece of work is ready for review and to talk about guidelines and deadlines for the next stage of the project.

A: Hi B. This is A. How are you?

B: Hola A. Estoy muy bien, gracias. ¿Cómo va el trabajo en el proyecto?

A: Really well. I'm actually calling to let you know that the first draft of the report is finished and ready for you to review. I've uploaded the file to our shared folder on the cloud server. I'd really appreciate your feedback when you have time to take a look.

B: Oh, eso es genial. Bien hecho por haberlo completado antes de lo previsto. Estoy a tope de trabajo esta tarde, pero voy a revisar el documento mañana a primera hora y te enviaré mis comentarios.

A: Thanks, I really appreciate it. I'll block out tomorrow afternoon to put through any amendments you'd like me to make.

B: Excelente. Gracias.

A: In the meantime, are you happy for me to start work on drafting the sales leaflets and the copy for the marketing emails?

B: Si, por favor comienza con ellos. ¿Tienes toda la información que necesitas?

A: Actually no. I've got all the background information but I'll need the specifics of the deal you want to promote in the leaflets and emails. Can you provide me with the product launch dates and special pricing packages?

B: Oh, sí, voy a hacer que el equipo de marketing te envíe los datos por correo electrónico de inmediato.

A: Thank you.

B: Por cierto, vamos a necesitar dos versiones de cada correo electrónico - uno para los clientes existentes y otro para los potenciales nuevos que expresen interés a través de la página web. Serán muy similares, sólo el primer párrafo tendrá que ser diferente.

A: Right, ok. That's no problem. So what timescales are we working towards?

B: Tenemos un poco de tiempo para esto. ¿Puedes conseguirme los primeros borradores para el próximo martes?

A: Yes, sure. I'll get started now, and wait for your feedback on the report tomorrow.

DIALOGUE 16 • B

A is a freelance writer who is working on a project for B. She calls B to let him know that the first piece of work is ready for review and to talk about guidelines and deadlines for the next stage of the project.

A: Hola B. Habla A. ¿Cómo estás?

B: Hi A. I'm very well thanks. How is the work going on the project?

A: Muy bien. En realidad estoy llamando para hacerte saber que el primer borrador del informe está terminado y listo para tu revisión. He subido el archivo a nuestra carpeta compartida en el servidor de la nube. Me encantaría recibir tus comentarios cuando tengas tiempo de echarle un vistazo.

B: Oh that's great. Well done for getting that completed ahead of schedule. I'm flat out working on a proposal this afternoon, but I'll review the document first thing tomorrow and get back to you with my comments.

A: Gracias, te lo agradezco mucho. Voy a bloquear mañana por la tarde para trabajar en cualquier enmienda que quieras que haga.

B: Excellent. Thanks.

A: Mientras tanto, ¿te parece bien que comience a trabajar en la redacción de los folletos de ventas y en la copia de los correos electrónicos de marketing?

B: Yes, please make a start on those. Do you have all the information you need?

A: En realidad no. Tengo todos los antecedentes pero necesito los detalles del negocio que deseas promocionar en los panfletos y correos electrónicos. ¿Podrías darme las fechas de lanzamiento de los productos y de los paquetes de precios especiales?

B: Oh yes, I'll get the marketing team to email that data over to you right away.

A: Gracias.

B: By the way, we'll need two versions of each email – one for existing customers and one for new prospects who express interest through the website. They will be very similar, just the opening paragraph will need to be different.

A: Bien, ok. Eso no es problema. Entonces, ¿en qué plazos estaríamos trabajando?

B: We've got a bit of time on this one. Can you get me first drafts by next Tuesday?

A: Sí, seguro. Voy a empezar ahora mismo, y espero tus comentarios sobre el informe mañana.

DIALOGUE 17 • A

A has changed his mind about a purchase and wishes to return the item to the shop. B is the sales representative who explains that the store's policy is to offer credit or exchange but not refunds for change of mind purchases. A accepts an exchange.

A: Hi. I'm wondering if you can help me, please?

B: Sí, señor, ¿qué puedo hacer por usted?

A: I bought this shredding machine yesterday, but when I got it back to the office I realised it's not suitable.

B: ¿La máquina tiene alguna falla?

A: No, but it's just not robust enough for our needs. Apparently we need a secure cross-cut shredder, with the capacity to shred at least 20 pages at a time.

B: ¿Se ha utilizado esta trituradora?

A: No, it's still in the original packaging and as you can see it hasn't even been opened. And I have the receipt right here.

B: OK, gracias. Por desgracia nuestra política en la tienda es no ofrecer reembolsos por cambios de opinión. Sin embargo, le puedo ofrecer realizar un cambio o una nota de crédito de la tienda. ¿Eso sería aceptable para usted?

A: Yes, absolutely. Could you please show me some of your other shredders; hopefully you have something more suitable for us.

B: Por supuesto. Tenemos tres modelos de trituradoras de corte transversal. Estas dos son bastante pequeñas, pero esta toma hasta 25 páginas a la vez y es muy rápida. Hay un modelo más caro disponible también, que viene con un alimentador automático de papel, pero tendríamos que pedirlo ya que no lo tenemos en stock.

A: No thanks, this one looks ideal. How much is it?

B: Son $125, así que habría que abonar $54 adicionales si usted cambia la suya por esta.

A: That's fine. I'll take it.

B: Ok voy a procesar el cambio primero. ¿Podría por favor completar su nombre y dirección en este formulario? Y le pediré a mi gerente que lo firme. Luego podré tramitar la venta de la nueva máquina.

A: OK, thank you.

DIALOGUE 17 • B

A has changed his mind about a purchase and wishes to return the item to the shop. B is the sales representative who explains that the store's policy is to offer credit or exchange but not refunds for change of mind purchases. A accepts an exchange.

A: Hola. Me pregunto si usted me puede ayudar, ¿por favor?

B: Yes sir, what can I do for you?

A: Yo compré esta máquina trituradora ayer, pero cuando llegué a la oficina me di cuenta de que no es la adecuada.

B: Is the machine defective?

A: No, pero no es lo suficientemente robusta para nuestras necesidades. Aparentemente necesitamos una trituradora de papel segura, con capacidad para triturar al menos 20 páginas a la vez.

B: Has this shredder been used at all?

A: No, aún está en su embalaje original y, como puede ver, aún no se ha abierto. Y tengo el recibo aquí.

B: OK, thank you. Unfortunately our store policy is not to offer refunds for change-of-mind purchases. I can offer you an exchange though, or a store credit note. Would that be acceptable?

A: Sí, absolutamente. ¿Me podría mostrar algunas de sus otras trituradoras? A lo mejor haya algo más adecuado para nosotros.

B: Certainly. We have three models of cross-cut shredder. These two are quite small, but this one takes up to 25 pages at a time and is very fast. There's a more expensive model available too, which comes with an automatic paper feeder, but we'd have to order that in for you as it's not in stock.

A: No, gracias, ésta parece ideal. ¿Cuánto cuesta?

B: It's $125, so there would be an additional $54 to pay if you exchange yours for it.

A: Muy bien. Me la llevo.

B: OK, I'll just process the return for you first. Could you please fill in your name and address details on this form, and I'll get my manager to sign it off. Then I can process the sale of the new machine.

A: OK, gracias.

DIALOGUE 18 • A

A is looking for a financial advisor and calls an accounting firm to learn more about their services. B is the business development manager who answers A queries and arranges to meet with him.

A: Hi, you're through to A Jackson. I'm the business development manager here at Accounting Associates. I understand you're looking for some information about our services?

B: Hola A. Sí, por favor. Su recepcionista dijo que usted sería la persona adecuada para hablar sobre las cuentas de mi negocio.

A: I certainly am. Before we get started, could I ask your name please?

B: Si, soy B Green.

A: Thank you. And may I ask where you heard about us?

B: Sí, uno de sus clientes es amigo mío. Él me recomendó que lo llamara.

A: Oh that's good to hear. So you need help with your business accounts?

B: Sí. Acabo de lanzar mi propia empresa de consultoría y tengo que organizar toda mi contabilidad y facturación correctamente. Voy a necesitar ayuda con mis declaraciones de impuestos y reportes financieros también, y además podría utilizar algunos consejos de impuestos para asegurarme de haber estructurado todo correctamente.

A: We can help you with all of that. We specialise in accounting for small businesses and we can provide a complete bookkeeping service if you want it. Or if you'd prefer to take care of that in-house, we can help you choose and set up your accounting software and train you on how to use it efficiently.

B: Eso suena muy bien.

A: Would you like an appointment to come in and discuss it? I'd like to learn more about your business and talk you through our services and pricing structure. I can come to your offices, if that would be more convenient for you than coming here?

B: En realidad, nuestra oficina todavía se está terminando, por lo que prefiero ir a la suya, por favor. ¿Qué tal el jueves o el viernes? Alrededor de las 11 cualquiera de los dos días sería ideal para mí.

A: Let's make it Thursday. I'm putting it in my diary now. I look forward to meeting you.

DIALOGUE 18 • B

A is looking for a financial advisor and calls an accounting firm to learn more about their services. B is the business development manager who answers A queries and arranges to meet with him.

A: Hola, está comunicado con A Jackson. Soy el gerente de desarrollo de negocios aquí en Accounting Associates. Entiendo que usted está buscando un poco de información acerca de nuestros servicios.

B: Hi A. Yes, please. Your receptionist said you would be the right person to talk to about the accounts for my business.

A: Ciertamente lo soy. Antes de empezar, ¿podría indicarme su nombre, por favor?

B: Yes, it's B Green.

A: Gracias. ¿Y podría preguntarle cómo se enteró sobre nosotros?

B: Yes, one of your clients is a friend of mine. He recommended that I give you a call.

A: Oh, qué bueno escucharlo. ¿Así que usted necesita ayuda con sus cuentas comerciales?

B: Yes. I've just launched my own consulting firm and I need to get all my bookkeeping and invoicing set up properly. I'll need help with my tax returns and financial reports too, and I could also use some tax advice to make sure I've structured everything properly.

A: Nosotros le podemos ayudar con todo eso. Nos especializamos en la contabilidad de las pequeñas empresas y podemos proporcionar un servicio de contabilidad completa si usted lo desea. O, si prefiere realizarlo por su cuenta, podemos ayudarle a elegir y configurar su software de contabilidad y entrenarlo en cómo utilizarlo de manera eficiente.

B: That sounds great.

A: ¿Le gustaría hacer una cita para venir y hablar de ello? Me gustaría aprender más sobre su negocio y hablar sobre nuestros servicios y la estructura de precios. Yo puedo ir a su oficina, si es más conveniente para usted que venir aquí.

B: Actually our office is still being set up, so I'd rather come to you, please. How about Thursday or Friday? Around 11am on either day would be ideal for me.

A: Hagámosla el jueves. Lo estoy agendando ahora. Nos vemos, entonces.

DIALOGUE 19 • A

A is a secretary who has just realised he made a mistake in a document that has gone out to a client. B is his boss. A explains to B what has happened and how he proposes to rectify the error.

A: Hi B, have you got a moment. I need to talk to you about something.

B: Claro. Pase y tome asiento. Entonces, ¿cuál es el problema?

A: I've just been reading back over the project proposal we sent to the Myer client yesterday afternoon, and I've noticed an error. I'm so sorry, but it was totally my mistake. I should have proofread it more closely before sending it out.

B: ¿Cuál fue el error? ¿Es grave?

A: We used a template from another proposal as the basis for this document, and I'm afraid I left some of last year's data in place when I updated the financial section. Some of the totals don't add up correctly, and the sales projection figures are wrong.

B: Dios mío. Eso va a hacernos quedar muy poco profesionales.

A: Yes, I know. I'm so sorry. I feel really bad about it.

B: No se preocupe A. Al menos el error es sólo en la información de apoyo, no en el presupuesto ni en los parámetros del proyecto. Y todos corrimos para terminar ese documento y presentarlo en el plazo establecido. Este tipo de cosas sucede, y le agradezco que haya venido a avisarme con tanta prontitud. Entonces, ¿qué propone hacer al respecto?

A: Well I've already spoken to the client's secretary to explain my error, and she said that the project team haven't yet met to review the proposal. I've prepared an updated document with all the correct figures and she said she would make sure they receive the new version before their meeting, if I send it through this morning. Would you be happy for me to do that?

B: Sí. Aunque primero me gustaría revisar el documento corregido, por favor.

A: Yes of course. I've got a copy here for you to review.

B: Gracias, es un buen trabajo A. Es una pena lo del error, pero lo manejó muy bien. La llamaré una vez que haya leído este documento, para confirmar que lo puede enviar.

A: OK. Thanks for being so understanding. I'll be more careful next time.

DIALOGUE 19 • B

A is a secretary who has just realised he made a mistake in a document that has gone out to a client. B is his boss. A explains to B what has happened and how he proposes to rectify the error.

A: Hola B, ¿tiene un momento? Necesito hablar con usted sobre algo.

B: Sure. Come in and take a seat. So what's the problem?

A: Estaba releyendo la propuesta de proyecto que le enviamos al cliente Myer ayer por la tarde y me he dado cuenta de un error. Lo siento mucho, pero fue totalmente un error mío. Yo lo debería haber corregido más de cerca antes de enviarlo.

B: What was the error? Is it serious?

A: Nosotros utilizamos una plantilla de otra propuesta como base para este documento, y me temo que dejé algunos de los datos del año pasado cuando actualicé la sección financiera. Algunos de los totales no suman correctamente y las cifras de las proyecciones de ventas están equivocadas.

B: Oh dear. That's going to make us look very unprofessional.

A: Sí, lo sé. Lo siento mucho. Me siento muy mal por eso.

B: Don't worry A. At least the mistake is only in the supporting information, not in the quote or the project parameters. And we were all rushing to get that document finished and submitted by the deadline. This sort of thing happens, and I appreciate you coming to tell me so promptly. So what do you propose to do about it?

A: Bueno, yo ya he hablado con la secretaria del cliente para explicar mi error, y me dijo que el equipo del proyecto todavía no se reunió para revisar la propuesta. He preparado un documento actualizado con todas las cifras correctas y me dijo que iba a asegurarse de que ellos reciban la nueva versión antes de su reunión, si lo enviaba esta mañana. ¿Usted está de acuerdo en que lo haga?

B: Yes. I'd like to check over the revised document first though please.

A: Sí, por supuesto. Tengo una copia aquí para que lo revise.

B: Thank you, that's good work A. It's unfortunate about the mistake, but you handled this well. I'll call you once I've read through this document, to confirm you can send it.

A: OK. Gracias por ser tan comprensivo. Seré más cuidadosa la próxima vez.

DIALOGUE 20 • A

A is a business training consultant and B is the training manager at a small firm. B has sent an email enquiry and A is responding to try to sell him some services.

A: My name's A and I'm calling from Smart Business Training. You emailed us this morning about some training you're interested in, and I'd like to talk through how we can help you. Is now a good time?

B: Sí, estoy libre para hablar de eso ahora.

A: Great, so I see you're interested in our time management and productivity courses. Is the training for yourself?

B: No. En realidad soy el responsable de capacitación en una firma legal. Contamos con doce profesionales y dos miembros del personal administrativo que desean asistir a la capacitación. ¿Nos puede ofrecer un curso de formación en la empresa, o ellos tienen que asistir a alguno de sus talleres públicos?

A: Yes, we can come to you and give a private training session. Those are both half-day courses, so if you like we can combine them into a single full-day experience, to save on travel and set up costs.

B: Oh, sí, eso sería útil y menos problemático que estar atados al entrenamiento en dos días diferentes. Así que, ¿me podría comentar un poco más sobre los cursos?

A: Sure. We specialise in training for small professional firms, so the material is all tailored to businesses like yours. We focus on how to tackle the big issues all professionals face these days – constant distractions, email overload, and mastering the digital tools that can dramatically improve efficiency. We'll talk to you in advance about what software and email systems you use, so we can make sure everything is relevant.

B: Oh, eso suena muy bien. ¿Utilizan juegos de roles y situaciones en las capacitaciones?

A: Yes – and we prefer to use real-life examples from your own business for those, so that they'll resonate with your participants. Training is far more effective when it makes direct sense in the context of your work.

B: Sí, es cierto. Entonces, ¿qué pasa luego? ¿Ofrecen algún seguimiento de apoyo?

A: Actually, yes. We offer 2 weeks' free email coaching for all participants. They can contact us for expert advice if they have any questions about what they've learned, or if they want to talk through any difficulties that arise when implementing their learnings into their daily work.

B: Bueno, eso suena ideal. ¿Podría usted por favor enviarme un correo electrónico con los temas del curso y costos, y algunas fechas posibles en abril para el taller?

A: Yes, I'll send them through to you right away. Thanks for your time.

DIALOGUE 20 • B

A is a business training consultant and B is the training manager at a small firm. B has sent an email enquiry and A is responding to try to sell him some services.

A: Mi nombre es A y estoy llamando desde Smart Business Training. Usted nos envió un correo electrónico esta mañana sobre un tipo de capacitación que le interesa, y me gustaría conversar sobre cómo podemos ayudarle. ¿Ahora es un buen momento?

B: Yes, I'm free to discuss it now.

A: Genial, entonces, veo que usted está interesado en nuestros cursos de gestión y productividad de tiempo. ¿El entrenamiento es para usted mismo?

B: No. I'm actually the training manager at a legal firm. We have 12 professionals and 2 administrative staff members who would like to attend the training. Can you offer us an in-house training course, or will they need to attend one of your public workshops?

A: Sí, podemos ir a la empresa y darles una sesión de entrenamiento privado. Esos dos cursos son de medio día, así que, si quiere, podemos combinarlos en una sola sesión de todo el día, para ahorrar en viajes y costos.

B: Oh yes, that would be helpful, and less disruptive than having everyone tied up in training on two separate days. So can you tell me a bit more about the courses?

A: Claro. Nos especializamos en la formación de pequeñas empresas profesionales, por lo que el material es todo a la medida de empresas como la suya. Nos centramos en cómo abordar los grandes temas a los cuales todos los profesionales se enfrentan actualmente – las distracciones constantes, la sobrecarga de correo electrónico y el dominio de las herramientas digitales que pueden mejorar drásticamente la eficiencia. Vamos a conversar con usted de antemano acerca de los sistemas de software y de correo electrónico que utiliza, así nos aseguraremos de que todo sea relevante.

B: Oh that sounds great. Do you use role plays and scenarios in your training?

A: Sí, y preferimos utilizar ejemplos de la vida real a partir de su propio negocio, así son conocidos para sus participantes. La formación es mucho más eficaz cuando tiene sentido directo en el contexto de su trabajo.

B: Yes true. So what happens afterwards? Do you offer any follow up support?

A: En realidad, sí. Ofrecemos 2 semanas de entrenamiento gratuito por correo electrónico para todos los participantes. Pueden contactarnos para obtener asesoramiento de expertos si tienen alguna pregunta sobre lo que han aprendido, o si quieren hablar sobre de las dificultades en la aplicación de los aprendizajes en su trabajo diario.

B: Well that does sound ideal. Could you please email me the course outlines and costings, and some possible dates in April for the workshop?

A: Si, se los enviaré enseguida. Gracias por su tiempo.

DIALOGUE 21 • A

A wants to apply for a job. B is the recruitment consultant who answers his enquiry and talks him through the application process.

A: Right Job Recruitment, you're through to A.

B: Hola A. Mi nombre es B Black, y estoy respondiendo a un anuncio que acabo de ver en el sitio web BestJobs.com para un gerente de oficina en una empresa de contabilidad. Realmente me gustaría presentarme.

A: Hi B. Thanks for calling. I'm managing the shortlist for that position, so you've come through to the right person.

B: Genial. ¿Podría contarme un poco más sobre el trabajo, por favor?

A: Certainly. It's for a medium-sized firm in the city centre. They have about 80 employees based at the site, and the office is always busy with clients coming and going. They want someone very calm and professional, with solid experience in a similar environment. What's your background?

B: Suena ideal, en realidad. Actualmente soy el gerente de oficina en una firma legal con mucho trabajo. Tenemos alrededor de 40 profesionales y un gran equipo de personal de apoyo, incluyendo cinco recepcionistas para manejar a todas las visitas.

A: Interesting. So why do you want to leave that role?

B: Bueno, hace cuatro años que estoy aquí y estoy buscando un nuevo reto. Además, la ubicación no es la ideal - estamos bastante lejos de la ciudad en un parque empresarial, y estoy interesado en trabajar en un ambiente más vibrante.

A: It does sound like you could be a good candidate for this role. Can you please tell me about your education and experience?

B: Soy graduado en administración de empresas, y he estado en la gestión de empresas durante casi una década. Empecé como junior en una empresa de capacitaciones y luego fui promovido a gerente. Dejé esa posición después de tres años para tomar mi trabajo actual. Yo estaba listo para un desafío más grande y fue un gran paso en mi carrera.

A: OK great, so I'll need to see your CV and talk through some more details before I can put you forward, but based on this conversation it sounds like I'll be able to shortlist you. Have you got time to come in for a quick interview with me this afternoon?

B: Sí, seguro. Puedo llegar a sus oficinas alrededor de las 2pm.

A: Excellent. See you then.

DIALOGUE 21 • B

A wants to apply for a job. B is the recruitment consultant who answers his enquiry and talks him through the application process.

A: Right Job Recruitment, habla con A.

B: Hi A. My name is B Black, and I'm responding to an advert I've just seen in on the BestJobs.com website for an office manager at an accounting firm. I'd really like to apply.

A: Hola B. Gracias por llamar. Yo estoy gestionando la lista para esa posición, así que se ha comunicado con la persona adecuada.

B: Great. Can you tell me a bit more about the job please?

A: Por supuesto. Es para una empresa de tamaño medio en el centro de la ciudad. Tienen cerca de 80 empleados con sede en el lugar y la oficina está siempre ocupada con clientes que van y vienen. Quieren a alguien muy tranquilo y profesional, con una sólida experiencia en un entorno similar. ¿Cuál es su formación?

B: It sounds like a great fit, actually. I'm currently the office manager at a busy legal firm. We have around 40 professionals and a large team of supporting staff, including 5 receptionists to handle all the visitors.

A: Interesante. Entonces, ¿por qué quiere dejar ese cargo?

B: Well I've been here for four years and I'm looking for a new challenge. Plus the location isn't ideal – we're quite far out of town in a business park, and I'm keen to work in a more vibrant environment. I've been keeping my eye open for an exciting job in the CBD, and this opportunity looks ideal.

A: Ciertamente parece que usted podría ser un buen candidato para esta posición. ¿Podría comentarme algo acerca de su educación y experiencia?

B: I have qualifications in business administration, and I've been in office management for almost a decade. I started out as an office junior at a training company, then got promoted to manager. I left that role after three years to take on my current job – I was ready for a bigger challenge and it was a great career move.

A: OK genial. Tendré que ver su CV y conversar sobre algunos detalles más antes de que pueda presentarlo, pero en base a esta conversación, pareciera que podré incluirlo dentro de los favoritos. ¿Tiene tiempo para venir a una rápida entrevista conmigo esta tarde?

B: Yes, sure. I can get to your offices by about 2pm.

A: Excelente. Nos vemos entonces.

DIALOGUE 22 • A

A needs to rent some office space for a new business. B is the agent for a serviced office building, showing him the available space and demonstrating all the facilities.

A: Nice to meet you B. I'm A, the agent for the FreeSpace complex. Would you like to take a look around or do you have some questions first?

B: HolaA. Encantado de conocerlo. Vamos a echar un vistazo y le haré mis preguntas a medida que avanzamos

A: OK great. So we'll start here with the shared reception area. As you can see, it's very smart and it's staffed by a very professional reception team. I guess you met them when you first arrived?

B: Sí, fueron muy serviciales y amables. ¿Cuántos inquilinos hay en este complejo?

A: We have 16 office suites, and 12 are currently occupied, with another two companies moving in over the next month. Our tenants include lawyers, accountants and financial advisors, so it's a very busy and professional office. It's a great working environment.

B: Si, así parece.

A: This is the shared facilities area. As you can see, we have the very latest in digital office technology - multimedia projectors, teleconferencing facilities and state-of-the-art document centres with secure printing facilities. There are five meeting rooms plus a large boardroom, which are all free for tenants to use. You just have to book them through reception.

B: Impresionante. ¿Puedo ver una de las suites de oficina, por favor?

A: Yes, number seven here is available, or we have a larger unit available upstairs if you need more space. Each suite is fully equipped with ergonomic office furniture and cutting edge telecoms and wifi services.

B: Esto parece ideal. Entonces, ¿qué costos y cargos por servicio de alquiler debería esperar?

A: That will depend on the suite size and the length of the tenancy agreement. Let's just pop into my office and I'll show you the rental documents.

B: OK, gracias A.

DIALOGUE 22 • B

A needs to rent some office space for a new business. B is the agent for a serviced office building, showing him the available space and demonstrating all the facilities.

A: Encantado de conocerlo, B. Soy A, el agente del complejo FreeSpace. ¿Quiere echar un vistazo o tiene algunas preguntas primero?

B: Hi A. Great to meet you. Let's take a look and I'll ask my questions as we go.

A: Comenzaremos aquí con la zona de recepción compartida. Como puede ver, es muy elegante y está formada por un equipo de recepción muy profesional. Seguramente los conoció cuando llegó.

B: Yes, they were very helpful and friendly. How many tenants do you have in this complex?

A: Tenemos 16 suites de oficina y 12 están actualmente ocupadas. Otras dos empresas se mudarán el mes que viene. Nuestros inquilinos incluyen abogados, contadores y asesores financieros, por lo que es una oficina muy ocupada y profesional. Es un gran ambiente de trabajo.

B: Yes, it sounds like it.

A: Este es el área de instalaciones compartidas. Como puede ver, tenemos lo último en tecnología digital de oficina: proyectores multimedia, servicios de teleconferencia y centros de documentación último modelo con instalaciones de impresión segura. Hay cinco salas de reuniones, además de una gran sala de juntas, que son gratuitas para el uso de los inquilinos. Sólo tiene que reservar a través de la recepción.

B: Impressive. Can I see one of the office suites please?

A: Sí, la número siete está disponible, o tenemos una unidad más grande disponible arriba si necesita más espacio. Todas las suites están equipadas con mobiliario de oficina ergonómico y telecomunicaciones de avanzada con servicios wifi.

B: This looks ideal. So what rental costs and service charges can I expect?

A: Eso dependerá del tamaño de la suite y la duración del contrato de alquiler. Vayamos a mi oficina y le mostraré los documentos de alquiler.

B: OK, thanks A.

DIALOGUE 23 • A

A wants to get some business strategy advice but doesn't know who to ask. B is his accountant. B gives A some advice on what to look for and recommends a firm she has used before.

A: Hi B. This is A White. I'm just wondering if I could ask you for some quick advice.

B: Hola A, qué gusto saber de ti. ¿Cómo te puedo ayudar?

A: I'm getting ready to launch that business we discussed at our last review meeting, and I really need some guidance. I'm finding it really hard to put together my business plan and financial projections, and I'm just not sure that my marketing and commercialisation strategies are quite on track. I need to talk to a business consultant, but I have no idea who to turn to.

B: Oh, me alegro de que tus planes estén empezando a realizarse. Creo que tienes un gran concepto allí. Es una buena idea obtener algunos consejos en esta etapa. Mejor aún, empezar por el camino correcto desde el principio. A mí me parece que te iría bien con un mentor de negocios en lugar de con una firma de consultoría. Es alguien que va a trabajar contigo a largo plazo y que realmente llegará a conocer muy bien tu negocio.

A: Yes, I like the sound of that. I'd definitely rather deal with just one person.

B: Yo siempre creo que ese es el mejor camino a seguir para alguien como tú, que tiene una gran idea, pero no mucha experiencia en el lanzamiento o la gestión de una empresa. Un mentor se quedará contigo durante todo el viaje, y te ayudará con todos los retos que enfrentarás en los próximos años. Creo que eso es aún más importante en tu caso, ya que tú estás con deseos de entrar en un mercado de alta tecnología que se mueve rápidamente. Necesitarás a alguien a tu lado que te pueda ayudar a reaccionar a los cambios y a hacer evolucionar tu modelo y estrategia de negocio a medida que cambien las necesidades de los clientes.

A: Yes! That's exactly what I want. So can you recommend anyone?

B: En realidad yo conozco a alguien que creo que sería ideal. Él ha trabajado con un par de mis clientes en los últimos años y han hablado muy bien de él. Él realmente parece que se preocupa por las personas y las empresas con las que trabaja y ha manejado negocios exitosos él mismo por más de 30 años. Creo que realmente será capaz de ayudarte.

A: Great, can you email me his details please, and I'll give him a call right away. Thanks so much for your help Beatrice!

B: Es un placer. Me alegro de hablar contigo. ¡Buena suerte!

A: Thank you.

DIALOGUE 23 • B

A wants to get some business strategy advice but doesn't know who to ask. B is his accountant. B gives A some advice on what to look for and recommends a firm she has used before.

A: Hola B. Habla A. Me preguntaba si podría pedirte un consejo rápido.

B: Hi A, great to hear from you. How can I help?

A: Me estoy preparando para lanzar ese negocio que comentamos en nuestra última reunión de revisión y realmente necesito alguna orientación. Me está resultando muy difícil armar mi plan de negocios y proyecciones financieras y no estoy seguro de que mis estrategias de marketing y comercialización estén bien encaminadas. Necesito hablar con un consultor de negocios, pero no tengo idea sobre a quién recurrir.

B: Oh I'm glad that your plans are starting to come together. I think you've got a great concept there. It's a good idea to get some advice at this stage - far better to get on the right track from the start. It sounds to me like you'd be better off with a business mentor rather than a consulting firm – someone who will work with you for the long term, and really get to know your business well.

A: Sí, me gusta cómo suena eso. Sin duda es mejor tratar con una sola persona.

B: I always think that's the best way to go for someone like you, who has a great idea but not much experience in launching or running a business. A mentor will stick with you throughout the journey, and help you with all the challenges you'll face over the next few years. I think that's even more important in your case, since you're hoping to break into such a fast moving, high-tech market. You'll need someone by your side who can help you react to changes and evolve your business model and strategy as the needs of your customers change.

A: ¡Sí! Eso es exactamente lo que quiero. Entonces, ¿puedes recomendarme a alguien?

B: Actually I do know someone I think would be ideal. He's worked with a couple of my clients over the past few years and they've spoken extremely highly of him. He really seems to care about the people and businesses he works with, and he's been running successful businesses himself for over 30 years. I think he'll really be able to help you.

A: Genial, ¿me podrías enviar sus detalles por correo electrónico, por favor? Así lo llamo de inmediato. ¡Muchas gracias por tu ayuda B!

B: My pleasure. Lovely to talk to you. Good luck!

A: Gracias.

DIALOGUE 24 • A

A is a marketing consultant who has worked with B in the past. They haven't had any contact in a while so A calls to find out if there is anything B needs, and to inform her of her new services

A: Hi B, this is A from Expert Marketing. It's been a while since we spoke, so I just thought I'd call and see how everything's going for you.

B: Hola A. Qué bueno saber de ti. ¿Cómo estás?

A: I'm well thanks B. So what's been happening? Is business going well?

B: En realidad sí, hemos estado muy ocupados últimamente. La campaña publicitaria realmente ha dado sus frutos y los materiales de promoción que tú creaste para nosotros han sido un gran éxito.

A: Oh I'm really glad to hear that. Have you made any progress with your website yet?

B: Sí, finalmente tenemos el sitio en línea, pero me temo que no hemos hecho mucho con él todavía. Está en mi lista de cosas por hacer, pero no estoy muy segura de por dónde empezar, para ser honesta.

A: Oh. Well I was actually calling to let you know about a new service we've just launched, which sounds like it might be of interest to you in the circumstances. We've just hired an marketing specialist, and we're offering a new suite of digital services for small businesses like yours. We can help you with optimising your website, content marketing and managing your social media accounts.

B: Suena interesante. Entonces, ¿cómo es que eso genera negocios?

A: It's a powerful new strategy for generating business leads. It involves creating content for your website that will attract visitors who need the kind of services you offer. It can be blog posts, free downloads, white papers, videos and so on. Images and multimedia content are very popular at the moment. Sharing useful information on relevant topics shows people that you have something of value to offer them.

B: Genial. Suena como justo lo que necesitamos. ¿Podrías venir a una reunión para contarme sobre eso? ¿Estás libre a las 2 pm el viernes por la tarde?

A: Absolutely. I'll see you then. Thanks.

DIALOGUE 24 • B

A is a marketing consultant who has worked with B in the past. They haven't had any contact in a while so A calls to find out if there is anything B needs, and to inform her of her new services

A: Hola B, habla A, de Expert Marketing. Ha pasado un tiempo desde que hablamos, así que pensé en llamarte y ver cómo te está yendo.

B: Hi A. Good to hear from you. How are you?

A: Estoy bien, gracias B. Entonces, ¿cómo te ha ido? ¿Los negocios van bien?

B: Actually yes, we've been really busy lately. The advertising campaign has really paid off, and the promotional materials you created for us have been a huge success.

A: Oh, me alegro mucho de escuchar eso. ¿Has hecho algún progreso con tu sitio web ya?

B: Yes, we've got the site online at last, but I'm afraid we haven't done much with it yet. It's on my to-do list, but I'm not really sure where to start, to be honest.

A: Oh. Bueno, en realidad yo te estaba llamando para informarte acerca de un nuevo servicio que acabamos de lanzar, que creo que podría ser de tu interés en estas circunstancias. Acabamos de contractar a un especialista en marketing y estamos ofreciendo un nuevo conjunto de servicios digitales para las pequeñas empresas como la tuya. Nosotros podemos ayudarte con la optimización del sitio web, el marketing de contenidos y la gestión de tus cuentas de redes sociales.

B: Sounds interesting. So how does that generate business?

A: Bueno, el contenido atrae a la gente a tu sitio web, y luego tú recoges sus datos de contacto a cambio de descargas gratuitas. Es muy eficaz, ya que atrae a las personas que están realmente interesadas en lo que tienes para ofrecer, lo que lleva a una mayor calidad y mejores tasas de conversión.

B: Great. It sounds like just what we need. Could you come in for a meeting to talk me through it? Are you free at around 2pm on Friday afternoon?

A: Por supuesto. Nos vemos entonces. Gracias.

DIALOGUE 25 • A

A is the accounts clerk for a company and B is the client. A calls B to chase up payment on an unpaid invoice.

A: Accounts Department, A speaking.

B: Hola A. Habla B, de Expert Marketing. Me contacto con usted para preguntarle por una factura del mes pasado. ¿Es usted la persona indicada para hablar de esto?

A: Yes, I can help you with that. Do you have the invoice number to hand?

B: Sí, es INV-37601. Fue enviada el 17 de diciembre.

A: Just a moment, I'm just logging in to our payment system to check whether we have received it. What amount was it for?

B: $18 570.Fue por la estrategia de marketing de fin de año y la publicidad que compraron para las ediciones de Navidad de todas las revistas especializadas. Venció el 31 de diciembre y necesitamos el pago con urgencia para poder ajustar cuentas con esas publicaciones.

A: Ah yes, here it is. I see it was received on December 19th and sent to the Communications Department for authorisation. Let me just check if we ever received back the signed copy.

B: Gracias.

A: Oh it's right here in the pile for processing today. I'm so sorry for the delay - it looks like the Marketing Director has only just returned from vacation, as there's a whole stack of authorised invoices here. It must have been waiting on her desk all this time.

B: Oh, ya veo. ¿Entonces se pagará hoy?

A: Yes, I'll process it for priority payment immediately. The funds should be in your account by tomorrow morning.

B: OK, está muy bien, gracias, A. Le agradezco su ayuda.

A: It's my pleasure B. I'm so sorry the invoice wasn't paid on time.

DIALOGUE 25 • B

A is the accounts clerk for a company and B is the client. A calls B to chase up payment on an unpaid invoice.

A: Departamento de Cuentas, habla A.

B: Hi A. This is B from Expert Marketing. I'm just contacting you to enquire about an invoice from last month. Are you the best person to speak to about it?

A: Sí, lo puedo ayudar con eso. ¿Tiene el número de factura a mano?

B: Yes, it is INV-37601. It was sent on 17 December.

A: Sólo un momento, estoy ingresando a nuestro sistema de pagos para comprobar si la hemos recibido. ¿Por qué cantidad era?

B: $18 570. It was for the year-end marketing strategy and the advertising you purchased in the Christmas editions of all the trade magazines. It was due for payment by December 31, and we urgently need to take payment so we can settle accounts with those publications.

A: Ah, sí, aquí está. Veo que fue recibida el 19 de diciembre y se envió al Departamento de Comunicaciones para su autorización. Permítame comprobar si alguna vez recibimos la copia firmada.

B: Thank you.

A: Oh, está justo aquí, en la pila para el procesamiento de hoy. Lamento el retraso. Parece que el director de marketing acaba de regresar de vacaciones, ya que hay toda una pila de facturas autorizadas aquí. Debe haber estado esperando en su escritorio todo este tiempo.

B: Oh I see. So will it be paid today?

A: Si, la procesaré para el pago prioritario inmediatamente. Los fondos estarán en su cuenta mañana por la mañana.

B: Ok that's great, thank you A. I appreciate your help.

A: Es un placer, B. Lamento que la factura no se haya pagado a tiempo.